IMMIGRANTS
WHO TOOK A STAND

BY MICHAEL BURGAN

CAPSTONE PRESS
a capstone imprint

Capstone Captivate is published by Capstone Press, an imprint of Capstone.
1710 Roe Crest Drive
North Mankato, Minnesota 56003
www.capstonepub.com

Library of Congress Cataloging-in-Publication Data is available on the Library of Congress website.

ISBN: 978-1-4966-9543-7 (library binding)
ISBN: 978-1-4966-9677-9 (paperback)
ISBN: 978-1-9771-5445-3 (ebook PDF)

Summary: Some of the most important changes in American culture have been driven by people born outside the United States. Immigrants may come as refugees, as workers, or as students. They may come as children or as adults. Once here, many speak out for the rights of others or try to build a better country by working within the government. Some give money to good causes. Others point out problems that need fixing. Still others create art and music that give voice to the downtrodden. Here are 25 immigrants who have made a difference by taking a stand.

Image Credits

Alamy: Archivio GBB, 53, Historic Collection, 34; Courtesy of the Federal Bureau of Investigations: 51; Getty Images: Bettmann, 35, Culture Club, 19, VH1/Christopher Polk, 58; Library of Congress: 5 (top right, bottom left and right), 8, 9, 17, 21, 22, 31, 42, 44, 47; National Park Service: Statue of Liberty National Monument and Ellis Island, cover, 1, 5 (back); Newscom: ANP/Ruud Hoff, 49, Everett Collection, 50, Reuters/Mannie Garcia, 36, Richard B. Levine, 39, Sipa USA/Anthony Behar, 54, UPI Photo Service/Greg Whitesell, 40, UPI Photo Service/Steve Grayson, 14, ZUMA Press/Brian Cahn, 56; Shutterstock: Allison Peltzman, 59, Debby Wong, 28, Denis Makarenko, 10, Everett Collection, 7, Leonard Zhukovsky, 5 (middle left), 12, My Hardy (background texture), 9, 19, 35, 51, 59; Wikimedia: DoD, 5 (middle right), 25, U.S. Senate, 5 (top left), 26

Editorial Credits

Editor: Michelle Bisson; Designer: Kayla Rossow and Tracy Davies; Media Researcher: Svetlana Zhurkin; Production Specialist: Tori Abraham

Printed and bound in the USA. PO 3837

TABLE OF CONTENTS

INTRODUCTION

Immigrants come to the United States for many reasons. Some seek better lives for themselves and their children. They look for jobs or education they can't find in their homelands. Others come to get away from wars or harsh living conditions.

In the United States, these immigrants often try to serve their new country in some way. They might speak out for the rights of others. They sometimes try to build a better country by working for the government. They might give money to good causes. Or they might point out problems that need fixing. Here are 25 immigrants who made a difference by taking a stand.

Henry Kissinger

Mazie Hirono

John Shalikashvili

Martina Navratilova

Marcus Garvey

Emma Goldman

5

CHAPTER ONE

ARTISTS, AUTHORS, AND ATHLETES

Most people love a good story or beautiful art. They enjoy sports as well. Many immigrants have succeeded in those fields. And some have used their talents to try to make life better for other Americans.

JACOB RIIS

(1848–1914)
Born in Ribe, Denmark

During the 1880s, millions of immigrants flooded into the United States. In many cities, families crowded into tiny, dirty apartments. Many children worked to help their parents buy food and pay rent. Jacob Riis was a reporter and photographer who described the harsh conditions the immigrants faced.

Riis came to the United States in 1870 to find work. He struggled at first, taking odd jobs. Then he became a reporter in New York City. He saw that many immigrants suffered when they first came to America, as he had. Starting in 1887, Riis and a photographer went out to see how the immigrants lived. Later Riis took the pictures himself. These images were even more powerful than the words he wrote. They clearly showed how the immigrants of New York needed help to better their lives.

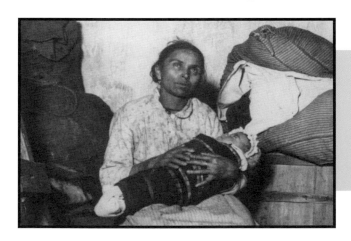

This 1889 photo of an Italian immigrant and her baby was one of many published in "How the Other Half Lives."

In 1889, people all over the country saw some of Riis's pictures in a national magazine. These pictures accompanied an article Riis wrote called "How the Other Half Lives." He later published a book of the same name. Riis became one of the country's first social reformers—someone who tries to help people who are homeless, hungry, or without jobs.

THOMAS NAST

(1840–1902)
Born in Landau, Germany

Political cartoons often poke fun at government leaders and important issues. The best cartoonists use one image and a few words to make their point. Thomas Nast has been called the "father of the American cartoon."

Thomas Nast made fun of everyone, including—in this self-portrait—himself!

Nast came to New York in 1846 as a 6-year-old. His family left Germany for political reasons. He studied art in his teens. When Nast was just 15, he began drawing for a newspaper. He first won fame during the 1860s. He worked for *Harper's Weekly*, a national magazine. Nast drew the first images of Santa Claus as an overweight, jolly man. He based "St. Nick's" big belly on his own! One of his most famous drawings of Santa was printed in 1881. That vision of Santa became part of American culture. Nast became even more famous for his drawings of Uncle Sam, the man who became a symbol of the United States itself.

This early cartoon of Uncle Sam shows him delivering money to the military.

Nast had a deep interest in politics. Starting in 1868, he targeted William "Boss" Tweed in many of his cartoons. Tweed was a major political figure in New York. He used his power to illegally make money for himself and his friends. Nast used his art to show the public that Tweed was breaking the law. At a time when many people in New York couldn't read, Nast's work helped them understand Tweed's crimes.

GETTING THE PICTURE

When Thomas Nast began drawing, taking photos was hard and expensive to do. Cameras were large, and producing an image required using messy chemicals. Newspapers and magazines then didn't have a way to print photos. Instead, they used art to help tell their stories. That's why Nast was able to get a job drawing for *Harper's Weekly*.

RUPERT MURDOCH

(1931–)
Born in Melbourne, Australia

In the 1990s, CNN was the world's most important cable news network. Rupert Murdoch wanted to change that. In 1996, he created Fox News to challenge CNN. His news network would broadcast 24 hours a day, as CNN did. But Murdoch wanted Fox News to be different. He believed millions of Americans wanted news that reflected their conservative beliefs. And Fox

By 2019, media mogul Rupert Murdoch had amassed a net worth of $7.35 billion.

News gave them that. By the 21st century, Fox News was the most popular cable news network in the United States.

Murdoch's father, Keith, owned two Australian newspapers. Rupert Murdoch took over the family business in 1954. He then began buying newspaper companies in several countries, including the United States. In 1974, he moved to America to expand his business. Murdoch bought 20th Century Fox. It was one of the world's major film companies. Murdoch used the Fox name for his new TV network as well.

The success of Fox News showed that many Americans welcomed Murdoch's conservative views. During the 2016 presidential election, more viewers tuned in to Fox News than any other network. And many of them supported the winner, Donald Trump. Today, Fox News plays a major role in shaping how Americans view the country's politics.

MARTINA NAVRATILOVA

(1956–)
Born in Prague, Czech Republic

On the tennis court, Martina Navratilova was one of the greatest players of all time. She won 18 Grand Slam singles titles, 31 Grand Slam women's doubles, and 10 Grand Slam mixed doubles. Off the court, Navratilova also made news. She was one of the first sports stars in the world to publicly say she was a lesbian. She then worked to promote the rights of women and all LGBT people.

When Navratilova was born, the Czech Republic was part of a larger nation called Czechoslovakia. Czechs didn't have the freedoms Americans enjoyed. They couldn't travel freely or move to other countries. But the Czech government let Navratilova go abroad to play because of her tennis skill. But the country didn't let her keep the money she earned. In 1975, Navratilova decided to remain in the United States after playing there. She wanted the freedom offered in America. She became a U.S. citizen in 1981.

That same year, Navratilova told the world she was gay. She faced prejudice because of this. But Navratilova was more interested in being honest about who she was. She continued playing in tennis championships until 2006. By then, Navratilova had been working to support the LGBT community. She helped create the Rainbow Card. Some of the money earned when people used this credit card went to the Rainbow Endowment, which donated the money to LGBT organizations.

DIKEMBE MUTOMBO

(1966–)
Born in Kinshasa,
Democratic Republic of the Congo

At 7 feet 2 inches (218 centimeters) tall, Dikembe Mutombo stands out in a crowd. He used his height and skill to become a star in the National Basketball Association (NBA). He ended his career with 3,289 blocked shots, the second highest ever in the league. But Mutombo won almost as much fame for his work helping others.

Dikembe Mutombo moves past an opposing player in one of the many games he played for the Atlanta Hawks.

Growing up, Mutombo was a tall, skinny kid and the target of neighborhood bullies. He excelled in school, though, and eventually learned to speak nine languages. At 16, he began playing basketball. In 1987, he entered Georgetown University in Washington, D.C., on a U.S. scholarship that aids people from other nations. By 1991, he was one of the top college players in the country. Mutombo entered the NBA that year. In 2015, he was elected to the Naismith Memorial Basketball Hall of Fame.

Mutombo began his humanitarian work while still in the NBA. In 1997, he created the Dikembe Mutombo Foundation. It built a hospital in Kinshasa. He also worked with Basketball Without Borders Africa. This organization encourages young Africans to play basketball. It also promotes health and education. In the United States, Mutombo joined the board of directors of the Centers for Disease Control (CDC) Foundation in 2014. Mutombo has won many awards honoring his humanitarian work.

DID YOU KNOW?

For the CDC, Mutombo made a video about Ebola, a deadly disease. It was shown in Congo to help people there take action to stop the spread of the virus.

CHAPTER TWO

GOVERNMENT SERVANTS

People can serve their country in many ways. That includes joining the military or entering government service. These immigrants showed their love for the United States by doing one or both of those things.

CARL SCHURZ

(1829–1906)
Born in Liblar (now Erftstadt), Germany

In 1848, Carl Schurz was one of many young Germans who rebelled and was arrested while fighting for a democratic Germany. Schurz escaped and fled to the United States in 1852. He became a lawyer in Wisconsin and joined the newly formed Republican Party. Like most Republicans, he opposed slavery.

Carl Schurz always stood up for those who couldn't easily speak for themselves.

After Abraham Lincoln became president in 1861, he asked Schurz to represent the U.S. government in Spain. Schurz agreed but soon returned to America so he could serve in the Union army during the Civil War (1861–1865). After the war, Schurz settled in Missouri. In 1868, voters there elected him to the U.S. Senate. He was the first ever German American senator.

After serving in the Senate, in 1877, Schurz joined the cabinet of President Rutherford B. Hayes. The cabinet is made up of the heads of various government agencies. They advise the president. As secretary of the Department of Interior, Schurz's duties included preserving the country's natural resources.

Schurz was the first immigrant in more than 50 years to serve in a presidential cabinet. He left government service in 1881 and fought to improve how government workers were hired. Schurz thought workers should be chosen because they had the best skills for the job, not because they personally knew political leaders.

A FIGHT FOR FREEDOM

Germany in 1848 was a collection of states and cities, not a united country. Across Germany, small groups of wealthy and powerful people ruled. Average Germans could not elect their leaders. They also lacked freedom of speech and religion. Carl Schurz joined many other Germans who wanted change. Their efforts are called the German Revolution of 1848. In some cities, the rebels battled government forces. Schurz and others came to America when they saw that German leaders would not give them the freedoms they sought. Throughout the 1800s, more than 5 million Germans came to the United States.

People who fought for democracy in Germany in 1848 were attacked by government forces.

FELIX FRANKFURTER

(1882–1965)
Born in Vienna, Austria

Lawyer Felix Frankfurter believed the United States needed an organization to protect the rights spelled out in the U.S. Constitution. So, in 1920, he helped found the American Civil Liberties Union (ACLU) to do just that. Almost two decades later, Frankfurter began playing a part in deciding what the Constitution means. He was named a justice of the U.S. Supreme Court.

Frankfurter came to the United States with his family as a 12-year-old in 1894. They were escaping prejudice against Jewish people. But Frankfurter didn't entirely escape that in the United States. When he graduated from Harvard Law School, he was the top student in his class. He briefly worked for a major New York law firm. Because of prejudice against Jewish Americans, the firm suggested he change his name, which reflected his Jewish background. Frankfurter refused and left the firm.

When Felix Frankfurter was appointed to the Supreme Court, he faced opposition because he was an immigrant.

When Franklin D. Roosevelt became president in 1933, he sometimes received advice from Frankfurter. The two had known each other for many years. In 1939, Roosevelt appointed Frankfurter to the U.S. Supreme Court. In 1948, Frankfurter hired the first Black lawyer to serve as a clerk for a Supreme Court justice. Six years later, Frankfurter joined the other justices in ruling against segregation in U.S. schools. Frankfurter served on the Court until 1962.

HENRY KISSINGER

(1923–)
Born in Fürth, Germany

   Before World War II (1939–1945) started, many Jewish families fled Germany. The country's leader, Adolf Hitler, had taken away Jewish people's rights. During the course of the war, he ordered the killing of 6 million Jewish people. He imprisoned many more. Henry Kissinger and his family were among the Jewish people who left Germany to survive. The Kissingers arrived in New York in 1938. Five years later, Kissinger became a U.S. citizen. He served in the army during World War II.

Though long retired, politicians and journalists still seek out Henry Kissinger for his opinion on foreign affairs.

After the war, Kissinger studied and then taught at Harvard University. He focused on government and international affairs. In 1969, he became the national security advisor to President Richard Nixon. In that role, Kissinger advised the president on how to keep the country safe. At the time, the country was involved in a long war in Vietnam.

In 1973, Nixon made Kissinger head of the State Department, which handles relations with foreign countries. Kissinger helped end America's role in the Vietnam War (1955–1975). For that, he won the Nobel Peace Prize. Nixon left office in 1974, but the new president, Gerald Ford, kept Kissinger on as secretary of state. He held that position until 1977.

DID YOU KNOW?

Twenty-one Americans or U.S. groups have won the Nobel Peace Prize. Henry Kissinger was the first immigrant to the U.S. to receive the honor.

JOHN SHALIKASHVILI

(1936–2011)
Born in Warsaw, Poland

During the Vietnam War, Major John Shalikashvili (pronounced shally-cash-veal-ee) was in the middle of the action. In 1969, he won a medal for his bravery during an enemy attack. He remained in the military after the Vietnam War ended. In 1993, Shalikashvili became the first immigrant to lead the Joint Chiefs of Staff. In that position, he was a top military advisor to President Bill Clinton.

Shalikashvili first experienced war at an early age. He was a boy in Warsaw when World War II began. In 1944, residents of that city fought the Germans who controlled it. The Germans crushed the revolt, and the Shalikashvilis left Warsaw. In 1952, they moved to Illinois. As a teenager, Shalikashvili learned to speak English in part by watching American movies.

After Vietnam, Shalikashvili earned the rank of general. In 1991, he led U.S. efforts to help Kurds in Iraq who had left their homes during the Gulf

Though John Shalikashvili rose to the top of the military ranks, he never forgot those at the bottom.

War (1990–1991). Shalikashvili arranged to bring food to the Kurds. He also helped hundreds of thousands of them safely return home. As chairman of the Joint Chiefs of Staff, Shalikashvili tried to improve pay and living conditions for lower-ranking troops. He retired in 1997 and was awarded one of the country's highest honors, the Presidential Medal of Freedom.

MAZIE HIRONO

(1947–)
Born in Fukushima, Japan

Throughout her political career, Mazie Hirono has achieved several historic "firsts." With her election to the U.S. Senate in 2012, she became the first Asian immigrant to serve in that branch of Congress. She was also the first Asian American woman elected to the Senate.

Mazie Hirono has worked tirelessly to make sure everyone has health care and protection from abuse.

Hirono was seven years old when she left Japan with her mother and a brother to escape an abusive father. They sailed to Hawaii, and Hirono's mother worked hard at low-paying jobs to help the family survive. Hirono helped by delivering newspapers.

After graduating from the University of Hawaii, Hirono went to law school in Washington, D.C. Soon afterward, she returned to Hawaii and entered politics. She won several state elections. In 2006, voters elected her to the U.S. House of Representatives. She served there six years before her election to the U.S. Senate.

Hirono has strongly supported the Affordable Care Act, which ensures that Americans get basic health care treatment. Her own battle with cancer in 2017 made her even more passionate about protecting the law. She has also worked to promote the interests of immigrants, women, and members of the LGBT community. She has been particularly concerned about protecting women who have been abused.

PREET BHARARA

(1968–)
Born in Firozpur, India

For eight years, some people who worked on Wall Street feared Preet Bharara. They knew he would be after them if they broke the law. Wall Street is home to many large banks and other companies that invest money. From 2009 through early 2017, Bharara was the U.S. attorney for the Southern District of New York, which includes Wall Street. His job included going after people who broke financial laws.

Preet Bharara has written a book called *Doing Justice* about his time in government.

Soon after Bharara was born, his family moved to the United States for more opportunity. At a young age, he decided to become a lawyer. After graduating from law school in 1993, he worked for private law firms. In 2000, he became a U.S. government lawyer in New York. He went after drug dealers and members of organized crime rings. In 2009, President Barack Obama named Bharara a U.S. attorney. Soon Bharara was managing more than 200 other government lawyers.

Bharara's office went after terrorists, illegal arms dealers, and computer hackers. Bharara also investigated Democratic and Republican politicians, as well as businesspeople, for corruption. Because of his work, for example, JPMorgan Chase Bank paid back $1.7 billion to settle charges that it had failed to act to prevent fraud. Also, some politicians lost their positions.

CHAPTER THREE

SOCIAL REFORMERS AND EDUCATORS

All countries have problems. Social reformers try to bring attention to these problems and help solve them. Often, ensuring people receive a good education is one way to address those issues. These immigrants used their skills to tackle problems and help others.

JOHN MUIR

(1838–1914)
Born in Dunbar, Scotland

When Americans explore the beauty of Yosemite or other U.S. national parks, they can thank John Muir. He helped create some of the first national parks. Muir wanted others to share his love of the outdoors and see the value of preserving its beauty.

John Muir (right) explored Yosemite Valley with President Theodore Roosevelt in 1903. That trip deepened Roosevelt's understanding of why nature had to be protected.

Muir came to the United States with his family in 1849 when he was 11 years old. His father wanted to join a religious congregation. The family settled in Wisconsin.

In the late 1860s, Muir began traveling across the United States. In California's Sierra Nevada mountains, he saw how cattle and sheep ranching were destroying fields and forests. That led Muir and Robert Underwood Johnson to take action. They pushed for creating Yosemite National Park in 1890. Two years later, Muir and others who shared his love of nature created the Sierra Club. The organization, which protects land and wildlife, continues its work today.

Muir's work caught the eye of President Theodore Roosevelt. In 1903, he and Muir went camping together in Yosemite. After the trip, Roosevelt became a great defender of natural lands. He signed laws that created new national parks and forests. Muir's writings about nature are still widely read.

PAULINE AGASSIZ SHAW

(1841–1917)
Born in Neuchâtel, Switzerland

Coming from a family that valued education, Pauline Agassiz Shaw devoted much of her life to helping others learn. She especially focused on immigrants. She wanted them to succeed in America.

Shaw's father was a famous Swiss scientist named Louis Agassiz. In 1848, he went to Massachusetts to teach at Harvard University. He decided to stay because of the greater opportunities for his research. Two years later, Shaw and her siblings joined their father in America. At 19, Shaw married a wealthy Boston investor. After becoming a mother, she started a school for her children and their friends. She then expanded her educational efforts. Starting in the 1870s, she opened the first public kindergartens in Boston. She used her own money to do it. Later, the city took over the schools and founded others. Shaw also wanted to help immigrant mothers who needed to work, so she set up nurseries where they could safely leave their young children.

The Pauline Agassiz Shaw vocational school was the first such school in the United States.

In 1881, Shaw shifted her focus to adult immigrants. She opened the North Bennet Street School, where newly arriving immigrants could learn trades such as woodworking. It was the first vocational school in the United States. Over time, the school added classes for children, sponsored recreational activities, and offered night classes for working adults.

SPECIAL HOUSES FOR IMMIGRANTS

One way Pauline Agassiz Shaw helped immigrants was by opening what were called neighborhood, or settlement, houses. Immigrants came to the houses to get help finding places to live and work, and to receive educational services. These houses sprang up in many U.S. cities. By 1910, there were 400 across the country.

Nurses came to help immigrant children who lived in the settlement houses.

ELIE WIESEL

(1928–2016)
Born in Sighet, Romania

Elie Wiesel never went into battle, but he knew the horrors of World War II. At 15, Wiesel and his family were sent to Auschwitz because they were Jewish. This was one of several death camps run by Nazi Germany. The Germans killed millions of Jewish people, and others they considered inferior, at these camps. Unlike his parents and one of his sisters, Wiesel was fortunate—he survived his time in the camps. But he never forgot what he and other Jewish people experienced during the war.

Elie Wiesel never stopped speaking out against prejudice. Here, he speaks at the 10-year anniversary of the Holocaust Museum, which honors the 6 million Jewish people killed by the Nazis during World War II.

At the end of the war, Wiesel went to France. He attended college and became a journalist. Wiesel came to the United States in 1955. He became famous after writing *Night*, a book about his experiences at the death camps. It was published in the United States in 1960. Wiesel's book helped the world understand how Jewish people had suffered during the war.

During the 1970s, Wiesel began teaching at U.S. universities. He continued writing books. He also worked to defend Jewish people and others who faced hatred because of their race, religion, or ethnic background. In 1986, he was awarded the Nobel Peace Prize.

DID YOU KNOW?

Germany's mass killing of Jewish people was called the Holocaust. Six million Jewish people died. Germans also killed people called Romani, gay people, and other Germans who opposed their government.

EDWARD SAID

(1935–2003)
Born in Jerusalem, Israel

Edward Said believed Arabs called Palestinians should have their own country. But the land they wanted was part of or controlled by Israel. Palestinians and Israelis have often fought over the land. Some people accused Said of supporting terrorism against Israel. But Said believed many of those people ignored the violence Israel sometimes carried out against Palestinians.

Said was born in Jerusalem before Israel became an independent country. He came from a wealthy Palestinian family. In 1951, his parents sent him to school in the United States. Said remained in the country for college, then taught at Columbia University in New York City. In 1978, he wrote a book called *Orientalism*. Said argued that some scholars in Europe and North America treated Arabs unfairly. When *Orientalism* came out, Said was actively working for Palestinian rights. He joined the Palestine National Council in 1977. This group represented the interests of many Palestinians who wanted their own country.

Edward Said was a strong champion of the right of Palestinians to have an independent nation.

Said was also an expert pianist. In 1999, he joined with Israeli musician David Barenboim to start the West-Eastern Divan Orchestra in Germany. Its goal was to help Israelis and Arabs better understand each other by playing music together.

HARRY HONGDA WU

(1937–2016)
Born in Shanghai, China

When Harry Hongda Wu moved to the United States, he spoke out against the brutality of the Chinese communist government.

For decades, China's communist government has kept tight control over what its people can say or do. Harry Hongda Wu learned that in 1960. He was arrested for his criticism of another communist government and was sent to a labor camp. In Chinese, the system of camps is called *laogai*.

Chinese communists accused Wu of being a threat to the government. He and other laogai prisoners were forced to work long hours and received little food. Wu suffered broken bones and weighed just 80 pounds (36 kilograms) when he was released in 1979. Six years later, he came to the United States. He began telling the world about the conditions in the Chinese labor camps.

Wu went back to China to secretly record the conditions in the camps. These videos were shown on TV in the United States and Great Britain. On a trip to China in 1995, Wu was arrested before being sent back to the United States. By then, Wu was a U.S. citizen and had founded the Laogai Research Foundation. Its goal was to convince other countries to pressure China to end the laogai system.

CHAPTER FOUR

PROTESTERS AND SOCIAL ACTIVISTS

At times, people think problems are so bad in a country they need to break the law to try to fix things. Or they take other strong steps to draw attention to their causes. Several notable immigrants have turned to this kind of protesting to help others.

MARY HARRIS "MOTHER" JONES

(1837–1930)
Born in County Cork, Ireland

Mother Jones led a march from Philadelphia to Long Island, New York, in 1903. Called the "Children's Crusade," its purpose was to bring attention to the terrible conditions for children working in the textile mills.

In the late 1800s and early 1900s, workers across the United States joined unions. These groups fought for better pay and working conditions. Mary Harris "Mother" Jones supported the workers. Her concern for working people earned Jones her nickname.

Jones and her parents left Ireland when she was 10 to escape starvation from the Irish Potato Famine. In 1867, Jones was living in Memphis, Tennessee, when a disease killed her husband and children. She moved to Chicago, and then the Great Fire there in 1871 destroyed a business she had started. Instead of feeling sorry for herself, Jones began helping workers fight for their rights. She often joined these protests in which workers sometimes refused to work. By the 1890s, she was helping coal miners form unions and supporting workers who made steel and cloth.

Jones's efforts took her all over the country. They also sometimes led to her being arrested. Company owners and the people who supported them thought unions and people like Jones were harmful to business. Putting Jones in jail was one way to prevent her from helping unions. Jones also opposed child labor. During the early 1900s, children sometimes worked 60 hours a week in factories and mines.

EMMA GOLDMAN

(1869–1940)
Born in Kovno, Lithuania

Emma Goldman's photo was taken right before she was deported.

Emma Goldman's beliefs shocked many Americans. She was an anarchist—someone who thinks laws and government limit people's freedoms. In writings and speeches, Goldman attacked the idea that people need religion, private property, or government. By seeking to do away with what many Americans cherished, Goldman made enemies.

At 16, Goldman and her sister came to America for a better life. Goldman soon became an anarchist and strongly defended workers' rights. At the time, most Americans worked 10 or more hours per day—often six or seven days a week—for low wages. By the early 1900s, Goldman was one of the few women in the United States who wrote and spoke for workers' rights.

Goldman also called for equal rights for women and greater freedom of speech. She hated that police could barge into her lectures and force her to stop talking, even though the First Amendment gave her the right to speak. Goldman also opposed war, and she spoke out against America's role in World War I (1914–1918). In 1917, she encouraged young men to resist the draft. For that, she was arrested and deported.

MARCUS GARVEY

(1887–1940)
Born in Saint Ann's Bay, Jamaica

The enslavement of Black people in the United States had ended by the time Marcus Garvey arrived. But Black people in the country lacked equality. Garvey fought to change that.

Garvey came to the United States in 1916 to continue the fight for equality. At first, he thought Black people could win equal rights by studying and working hard and avoiding politics. But he soon changed his mind. Black people could not wait for white Americans to help them. They had to take steps on their own.

In 1917, Garvey started the Universal Negro Improvement Association to reach that goal. He also believed Black people had to take pride in their history and their skin color. He said, "black is beautiful."

Garvey started businesses so Black people would not have to spend money at white-owned companies. But legal issues at one of Garvey's companies led

Marcus Garvey believed that Black people should not wait for the help of white people in their fight for equality.

to his arrest in 1922. He was deported five years later because of those issues. But the organization he had built was an important step in equality. And his message of having pride in being a Black person returned during the civil rights movement of the 1960s.

YOKO ONO

(1933–)
Born in Tokyo, Japan

During the 1960s and 1970s, millions of people took to the streets to protest the Vietnam War. Yoko Ono took a different approach. In 1969, along with her husband, John Lennon, Ono stayed in bed for days. The couple wanted to draw attention to the need for peace. At the time, Lennon was a member of one of the world's most famous rock bands, the Beatles. In the decades that followed, Ono continued to work with Lennon and on her own to call for world peace.

Ono and her family spent time in the United States when she was a child. The family returned to America during the 1950s. Ono became an artist and a musician. While in London in 1966, she met Lennon. They settled in New York during the early 1970s.

Lennon was shot and killed in New York City in 1980. Ono continued to try to stop violence around the world. She designed Iceland's Imagine Peace Tower. It shoots up light beams in honor of Lennon and to remind people of the need for peace.

John Lennon and Yoko Ono spent their honeymoon protesting for peace.

STOKELY CARMICHAEL

(1941–1998)
Born in Port of Spain, Trinidad

During the 1960s, many Black people followed the teachings of Martin Luther King Jr. He called for using nonviolent methods to protect Black Americans' rights. He worked with white people who wanted the same thing. Stokely Carmichael didn't want to work with white people to achieve equality. He thought Black people had to unite and work for change on their own. Many agreed with him.

Stokely Carmichael became known as the leader of the "Black Power" movement.

Carmichael left Trinidad in 1952 and moved to New York to join his parents, who had already moved there. When he entered college in 1960, the civil rights movement was underway. It sought to end segregation and ensure equal rights for Black people. After college, Carmichael began working for a civil rights group called the Student Nonviolent Coordinating Committee (SNCC). In 1966, Carmichael became the group's leader.

Carmichael called for "Black Power." To many Black people, that meant working for economic and political power for themselves. But the idea of Black Power frightened many white Americans. They thought it meant unleashing violence against them. Carmichael's message was of Black pride. "We have to stop being ashamed of being black!" Carmichael said. But the FBI and CIA began following him. By 1969, Carmichael had moved to Guinea, in Africa. He sometimes returned to America to speak, but he spent most of the rest of his life in Guinea.

DYING FOR CIVIL RIGHTS

Across the South, state and local governments tried to make it hard, if not impossible, for Black people to vote. The governments forced them to pay poll taxes or prove they could read. In 1964, Stokely Carmichael traveled to Alabama to help Black people register to vote. The same year,

After three men were killed in Mississippi for their civil rights work, their car was found in the bushes.

two white men and one Black man doing the same work in Mississippi were killed by white people. Those deaths helped convince Congress to pass the Voting Rights Act of 1965. It outlawed the actions that kept Black people from voting.

CHAPTER FIVE

FIGHTING FOR IMMIGRANTS

No one knows the problems immigrants face better than other immigrants. They know the issues include prejudice and a denial of rights. These immigrants worked hard to end prejudice and to make sure immigrants were treated fairly.

MARIA FRANCESCA CABRINI

(1850–1917)
Born in Sant'Angelo Lodigiano, Italy

Maria Cabrini wanted to serve others in the name of God. In 1877, a few years after running an orphanage in her native Italy, she became a Roman Catholic nun. Known as Mother Cabrini, she received a great honor for her work in the United States. In 1946, she was the first U.S. citizen named a saint by the Roman Catholic Church.

Mother Cabrini spent her life helping orphans.

In 1880, Cabrini and several other nuns started a religious order called the Institute of the Missionary Sisters of the Sacred Heart of Jesus in Italy. Cabrini's dream was to go to China to spread her faith. But in 1889, Pope Leo XIII sent her to the United States instead. He was the leader of the Catholic Church, and he wanted her to help the Italian immigrants arriving there. In New York City, Cabrini started schools and orphanages. As word spread about Cabrini's good works, other countries asked her to work with their people who needed help.

In 1909, Cabrini became a U.S. citizen. During her career, Cabrini founded a total of 67 schools, hospitals, and orphanages. Today, the Catholic Church considers her the saint who protects immigrants.

BAMBY SALCEDO

(1970–)
Born in Guadalajara, Mexico

Growing up in Mexico, Bamby Salcedo hung out with tough kids who robbed people and did drugs. She also discovered that she felt like a girl, though she was born a boy. Later, after coming to the United States, Salcedo began to help other transgender people

Bamby Salcedo has worked with the Elton John AIDS Foundation to help the LGBT community.

overcome the many problems they face. They often struggle in a society that doesn't understand what it's like for someone who is born one gender but identifies as another.

In her teens, Salcedo got into trouble with the police and fled Mexico to move to Los Angeles. At 19, she began making the transition from male to female. She had trouble with drug abuse. But around 2000, Salcedo changed her life. She got sober and went to college. Then she began to help other transgender people.

In 2009, Salcedo started the TransLatin@ Coalition. The group focuses on transgender Latinx immigrant women. It aims to improve health care for those women and protect their civil rights. Salcedo and her organization are also concerned with how Immigration and Customs Enforcement (ICE) treats trans women. Some have reported being abused or otherwise treated badly after being arrested.

In 2018, the TransLatin@ Coalition won national attention when it hung a banner during Game 5 of Major League Baseball's World Series. The banner read, "Trans People Deserve to Live."

CRISTINA JIMÉNEZ MORETA

(1984–)
Born in Ecuador

Cristina Jiménez Moreta was among the millions of immigrants who had come to the United States illegally. Without legal rights to be in the country, Moreta and her family always faced the fear that they could be deported. As an adult, Moreta decided she had to speak up for undocumented immigrants.

Cristina Jiménez Moreta is devoted to helping immigrants in the United States.

In Ecuador, Moreta's parents had struggled to find work, and violent gangs roamed city streets. So, when Moreta was 13, the family came to the United States and settled in Queens, a borough of New York City. Moreta learned to speak English and earned two college degrees. In 2004, she spoke publicly for the first time about being undocumented.

Moreta helped start United We Dream in 2008 and became its leader. The group helps young immigrants and their families. In 2012, Moreta asked President Barack Obama to protect DREAMers. That nickname was given to undocumented immigrants who came to the United States as children and wanted to stay. Obama signed an order giving qualified young immigrants the legal right to work and go to college. For her work helping young immigrants, Moreta received a MacArthur Fellowship in 2017. This "genius grant" was worth $625,000, and Moreta gave the money to United We Dream.

AMERICA'S DREAMERS IN 2018:

Most came from Mexico: 558,050
The largest population lived in California: 200,150
Average age (in years) when entering the U.S.: 6.1
Percentage working: 89

LORELLA PRAELI

(1988–)
Born in Ica, Peru

As a young girl, Lorella Praeli was hit by a car and her right leg was amputated. Her mother took her several times to the United States so Praeli could learn how to walk with an artificial leg. The trips, though, became difficult, and the Praelis moved to Connecticut. Praeli soon felt like a typical American kid. Only later did she learn that she was an undocumented immigrant and the problems that could cause.

Lorella Praeli has worked with many organizations to get help for immigrants.

In Peru, Praeli's mother had a good job. In Connecticut, she had to babysit and clean houses to earn money. Without the legal papers needed to buy a car, she had to walk to work. While in college, Praeli helped start an organization to assist undocumented students get money for school.

Praeli worked for Hillary Clinton's 2016 campaign for the presidency. Praeli focused on getting Latinx people to vote for Clinton. By then, Praeli was a U.S. citizen. After the 2016 election, Praeli worked for the American Civil Liberties Union (ACLU). She helped make sure immigrants weren't unfairly arrested or deported. In 2019, Praeli left the ACLU and became president of Community Change Action. Its goal is to improve the lives of low-income Americans, especially Black and Latinx people.

PROTECTING IMMIGRANTS' RIGHTS

From Felix Frankfurter to Lorella Praeli, immigrants have played an important role in the ACLU. In turn, the organization has often worked to defend immigrants' rights. In 1985, it started the Immigrants' Rights Project. The project not only goes to court to protect immigrants but also educates Americans about

Many marches have been held in the past several years in defense of immigrants' rights.

immigrants. For example, studies show that immigrants help create jobs by starting businesses and spending money.

TIMELINE

1868 Thomas Nast begins publishing cartoons that attack corrupt New York politician William "Boss" Tweed.

Carl Schurz becomes the first German American elected to the U.S. Senate.

1881 Pauline Agassiz Shaw opens the country's first vocational school in Boston to teach adult immigrants work skills.

1889 Jacob Riis publishes some of his pictures showing the harsh conditions faced by immigrants in New York.

1890 John Muir's work leads to the establishment of Yosemite National Park in California.

Mary Harris "Mother" Jones joins striking workers and helps them form unions.

1917 Emma Goldman is arrested for encouraging American men to resist the war draft.

Marcus Garvey starts the Universal Negro Improvement Association (UNIA) in New York.

1939 Felix Frankfurter joins the U.S. Supreme Court and serves on it until 1962.

1946 Mother Cabrini becomes the first U.S. citizen named a Roman Catholic saint.

1960 Elie Wiesel's book *Night*, which describes the horrors of the Holocaust, is published in the United States.

1966 Stokely Carmichael becomes the head of the Student Nonviolent Coordinating Committee (SNCC).

1969 Along with her husband, John Lennon, Yoko Ono takes part in a protest against the Vietnam War.

1973 Henry Kissinger wins the Nobel Peace Prize for his efforts to end the Vietnam War.

1981 Martina Navratilova, a champion tennis player, announces publicly that she's a lesbian.

1993 General John Shalikashvili becomes the first immigrant named head of the Joint Chiefs of Staff.

1995 Harry Hongda Wu is arrested in China for trying to document the conditions in the country's labor camps.

1996 Rupert Murdoch launches Fox News.

1997 Dikembe Mutombo starts a foundation to help people in his native country, the Democratic Republic of the Congo.

1999 Edward Said helps start the West-Eastern Divan Orchestra to help Israelis and Arabs better understand each other by playing music together.

2009 Preet Bharara becomes a U.S. district attorney and goes after terrorists and lawbreakers on Wall Street.

Bamby Salcedo starts the TransLatin@ Coalition to help transgender Latinx people.

2012 Mazie Hirono becomes the first Asian immigrant and the first Asian American woman elected to the U.S. Senate.

2017 Cristina Jiménez Moreta gives her $625,000 MacArthur Fellowship to United We Dream, an organization she started to help young undocumented immigrants.

2019 Lorella Praeli becomes president of Community Change Action, an organization that works to help low-income Americans, especially Black and Latinx people.

GLOSSARY

communist (KAHM-yuh-nist)—having to do with a political system in which goods and property are owned by the government and shared, and in which personal freedom is limited

conservative (kon-SUR-vuh-tiv)—favoring a small government, with few limits on how businesses are run

deported (di-PORT-id)—forced to leave a country by its government

humanitarian (hyoo-man-uh-TAIR-ee-uhn)—refers to actions meant to help others, or a person who performs those acts

Irish Potato Famine (EYE-rish poh-TAY-toe FA-muhn)—a time of starvation and death that devastated Ireland between 1846 and 1860 caused by a disease that destroyed potato crops

LGBT (EL GEE BEE TEE)—lesbian/gay/bisexual/transgender

prejudice (PREH-juh-dis)—dislike of a particular group, based on unfounded beliefs or opinions of that group

segregation (seg-ruh-GAY-shuhn)—the act of keeping one group of people separate from another, based on their race or ethnic backgrounds

transgender (tranz-JEHN-dur)—a person whose gender identity does not match the sex they were assigned at birth

undocumented (uhn-DAHK-yoo-mehn-tid)—lacking the papers to legally do something, such as enter a foreign country

vocational school (voh-KAY-shuhn-uhl SKOOL)—a school that prepares students for jobs that require special skills

READ MORE

Harris, Duchess, and Nina Judith Katz. *The Dreamers and DACA*. Minneapolis: Essential Library, 2018.

Kravitz, Danny. *Journey to America: A Chronology of Immigration in the 1900s*. North Mankato, MN: Capstone Press, 2015.

Nichols, Susan. *Famous Immigrant Politicians*. New York: Enslow Publishing, 2018.

INTERNET SITES

Biographies of Notable U.S. Immigrants
www.infoplease.com/us/immigration/biographies-notable-us-immigrants

Eastern European Immigrants in the United States
jwa.org/encyclopedia/article/eastern-european-immigrants-in-united-states

U.S. Immigration Timeline
www.history.com/topics/immigration/immigration-united-states-timeline

SOURCE NOTES

Page 8, "Father of the American cartoon . . ." "The Historic Elephant and Donkey," *New York Times*, August 2, 1908, https://timesmachine.nytimes.com/timesmachine/1908/08/02/106774821.pdf?pdf_redirect=true&ip=0, Accessed April 15, 2020.

Page 47, "Black is beautiful . . ." David Van Leeuwen, "Marcus Garvey and the Universal Negro Improvement Association," National Humanities Center, http://nationalhumanitiescenter.org/tserve/twenty/tkeyinfo/garvey.htm, Accessed April 15, 2020.

Page 51, "We have to stop . . ." Karen Grigsby Bates, "Stokely Carmichael, A Philosopher Behind The Black Power Movement," NPR, March 10, 2014, https://www.npr.org/sections/codeswitch/2014/03/10/287320160/stokely-carmichael-a-philosopher-behind-the-black-power-movement, Accessed July 13, 2020.

Page 55, "Trans people deserve to live . . ." Alanna Vagianos, "'Trans People Deserve To Live' Banner Flies at World Series Game," *HuffPost*, October 29, 2018, https://www.huffpost.com/entry/trans-people-deserve-to-live-banner-flown-at-world-series-game_n_5bd7032de4b0d38b5885a53a, Accessed April 15, 2020.

INDEX